TRANQUIL TRAVELS

SHARADA MURALIDHARAN

INDIA · SINGAPORE · MALAYSIA

ISBN

Hardcase 979-8-89777-268-1
Paperback 979-8-89699-995-9

I would like to thank my friends and family who have been with me through this journey, and have helped me complete these poems!

My special thanks to my husband, who patiently read my poems and gave his review. I thank my children and grandchildren for being my cheerleaders. Truly appreciate my sister for her continuous encouragement and support!

I dedicate this book to my parents who were my guiding light.

Sharada Murali

Contents

San Francisco, California

Celestial Dance

The day is winding down to a close,
Getting ready to say adios,
An exuberant blush, date night I suppose!
Oh! What a spectacular cosmic pose!!

Stage is set for a night time show,
The silvery moon will rise like a pro,
Stars ready for prom, will sparkle and glow,
Fireflies and comb jellies are primed to glint below!

Set your timer to the celestial beat,
Cycle of dawn and dusk is sure to repeat,
Mesmerized by the divine feat!
Oh my Creator! Your choreography is a sure treat!

Lido Key, Sarasota, Florida

Golden Hue!!!

Golden hue lights up the sky!
It's time to bid goodbye,
The gentle waves form little domes,
Busy birds head back to their homes.

Lights dimmed on sand castle,
Creatures hum to nestle...,
Little girls slow down their hustle,
Yes, It's time to wind down our bustle.

Golden hue gently fades,
Marvelous sky masquerades....
In hues of deep blue and grays,
Water shines in colorful sprays.

Bid farewell to a day well lived,
Stress and pressure all relieved
No more pain or sorrow....
Get ready for tomorrow!!!

Sarasota Beach, Florida

Shorebirds on the Seashore!!

Yip, yip, yippati, yips…..!!
High pitched calls of shorebirds zips…..
Black skimmers, snowy plovers everywhere…..
Forming a splendid fanfare! !

Shorebirds, standby in flawless row,
Awaiting the first streak of glow!
Looking up in east, in perfect peace,
Graciously heralding a new day at ease.

Doughty sea behind them roar,
Luminaries of hope, line up on shore
Dark skies span above in might,
Valiant birds sit tight, for the first ray of light!!!

Lido Beach, Sarasota, Florida

Dancing Doll!!

Dance little girl Dance!!
In this heavenly expanse!
Enjoy absolute bliss and trance!
I'm at awe seeing your prance!!!

The sugary white sand under your feet....
Your movements are well tuned to the beat .....
The skips and twirls are a gentle treat!
Your grace and poise is tranquil and neat!

Oh little girl! Who is staid!
Let your smile and joy always pervade,
Many glorious years to dance and parade!
Wishing you many accolades!!

Grimsby Drive, California

Call of Fall

Winter, an etching on the ground.
Spring, watercolors on sky abound,
Summer,a heavenly acrylic,
Fall, vibrant mosaic that's idyllic!!

Salubrious, crispy, cool breeze,
Land is getting ready for a freeze,
Leaves are turning yellow,red and brown....
A carpet of fallen leaves all around!

Aroma of pumpkin pie at its peak,
Fall winds caress our cheeks!
Crunching leaves under our feet.
Nature's color play, a sure treat!

Wind of change begins to blow,
Mountains , plains gearing up for snow!
Blast of colors in finale,
Mother Nature winding up the year's rally!

Can hear bells of transition ring,
Time for contemplation begin,
How mysterious is this fall?
That brings transformation in all!

Mitchell Park, California

Picture Frame

Picture perfect nature's frame,
Glory, Mystery is your name!
Folks are ready to sing thy fame,
Oh, no one can deny this claim!

Spruce, pine and oak stand up tall ,
Time or transitions, can't stall,
Grace and serenity in them all...
Mystifies us without a call!

Ponderous Clouds rest on hills behind.
Bring heaven and earth to a bind!
Oh, what a scene! One of the kind!
Where is the creator...? Where can I find...?

Palo Alto, California

A Cool Misty Morning!!

Little droplets of dew in air,
Panorama looks smokey and fair!
The sun begins its slow rise,
Ends its foggy disguise!

The world is shrouded in silence,
The waking day adorns a misty valance,
Nature seems to be at peace,
Until the fog begins to cease.

Swirling mist and stillness around,
Ease and serenity abound!
Cool fall winds gently kiss,
Dawn opens up a bliss!

Colorful leaves covered in haze,
Squirrels unravel the misty maze!
Splendid beauty, so divine!
Waiting for the sun to rise and shine!

Persimmons, Palo Alto, CA

Backyard Persimmons!!

Hanging like little lantern from tree,
Oh, what a glowing sight to see....!
You provide vivid colors in fall ,
A tasty winter fruit for all!

See you swing on tree straight and tall,
Sometimes rest on a willowy wall.
You hide behind glossy greens,
That turns into a fall blend of sheaves!

Blooms of white bells in summer,
Mellow to golden hearts, a true fall stunner!
Squirrels and Scrub Jays come to dine,
The fruity treat is deliciously divine!

You boldly display fall's beauty and transience.
A symbol of good luck and exuberance,
When Vibrant foliage departs in a melodrama,
You dazzle like holiday ornaments in a winter panorama!!

Grimsby Town, England

GTown Spruced with Pearls

Through the window one Morn,
Saw the birth of dawn!!
Driveway sprinkled with pearls,gleamed and shone!!
Ushering the season of giving on!!

Season begins, when the swallows all gone,
And sky's bright curtains drawn,
Watch white funfair as trees take a yawn!
All set for snowballs to glisten on green lawn!

Rays of golden hue from the eastern sky,
Strings the diamond crystals that glow and fly,
What a mighty jewel it is, that no one can ever buy!!
Seasons come to tease us, and soon bids goodbye!!

Through the hushed air falls the season's snow!
Bare white trees heavily bow,
Gives the season a silvery glow!
A pure delight! Oh my! What a show!!

Grimsby Town, England

A Crimson Blush

The fiery sun kisses the day goodbye
Crimson blush appears in the evening sky...
As lilac lights up the ether, so shy...
Time to snug in a bonfire nearby.

A picture perfect end to an autumn day,
Trees in black laces watch the color array,
A spectrum with no blues or grays,
Moment to thank and pray!

Heaven sprayed in pearly pink mallow,
Darkness waits for the last swallow,
Dust is gone, dawn is soon to follow,
Creator's artistry is a pure wallow!!

Palo Alto, California

Spectacular Autumn

Spectacular Autumn Celebration
Galore of colors, a classic decoration,
Nature at its best, pure exhilaration!
Oh Lord, What an exotic creation......!!!

Golden hue all around,
Montage of colors on the ground!
Western sky in amber! So profound...
Nature's glow and glamour astound!

Time to pause, cheer and acclaim!
Creator's Magnificent glory and fame!
Cherish the nature's beauty in flame,
Season of transition is never the same!

Palo Alto, California

Bird of Paradise

Bird, or a flower from the heavenly shrine?!
Your beauty is so pure, and divine!!
Sublime orange and the blue plumes,
Arranged in a perfect bloom!!!

In exotic vibrant colors you shimmer,
You unfold and blossom all summer!
Sunbirds flock to relish your nectar,
Crane flowers, a gift from the creator!!!

You look like a dazzling bird on flight,
Crowned in evergreen foliage, a splendid sight!
Symbol of immortality, beauty and might!
You bring any yard, an absolute delight!

San Jose, California

Squirrels!!

Squirrels up, down, scurry all around!!
See them on trees, see them on ground,
Shrubs and bushes they playfully surround!
Name a spot they can't be found!

Gracefully they scamper and leap,
Dreys and burrows places they sleep,
Under the leaves or ground, food they keep,
Can hear their squeak loud and deep!

Squirrels shine in many coats they wear,
Grey, red, and brown,colors they bear,
Diligence and prudence is what they teach,
Heed to them, triumph one is sure to reach!!

Vero beach, Florida

Vero Beach

Ocean waters so pristine,
A winter day so crisp and sheen,
Emerald waters kissing the heaven seen,
The gentle waves wash clean!

Surfers ride among the waves,
Paddler cruise merrily and brave,
Teens seen playing with Frisbees,
Children buzz around like bumble bees!

Sandpipers scurry by the water's edge,
Shells sprinkle the shore as the waves dredge,
Fishing tackle, line the shore by the ledge,
Seagulls circle above the waters with no hedge!

Warm waters lave our tired feet,
Soft winds nudge with a warm greet!
Perfect joy to hear the waves rhythmic beat!
This glorious day, a wonderful treat!

Grimsby Town, England

Wake Up Grimsby Town!

Night sky prepares to take rest,
Silver ball bids goodbye from the west,
The eastern sun trumpets the day's fest!
Oh, My! Nature's glory at its best!!!

Trees uncover the dark inky blanket,
Dreamy clouds remove their gray jacket,
Sky rolls out its bright blue carpet!
Daylight illuminates the mighty planet!!

Night sky whispers adieu, and wraps up,
Coral sky primed to glow and warm up,
Aromatic Earl Gray ready in a teacup,
Glorious blessed day is just starting up!!

California

Pure Beauty!!

Emerald green grass under your feet,
You gallop with no shoes, or cleats!
The trot is in a perfect rhythmic beat,
Watching with your sir, an amazing treat!

The trees lined up witness your gentle play,
Hikers stop to watch your groomed tail sway!
As horsemen canter you away,
Oh! What a magnificent, glorious day!

Black beauty, so glamorous, and tall,
Dark mane,white muzzles, you are a perfect doll!
Look perfectly groomed for the dance hall!
Enjoy your parade before you go to your stall!

California

A Magical Hike!!

Grandeur of nature is so magical!!
Jade carpet, sapphire mountain, just classical,
Silver beams from the horizon pure mystical,
This Magnificent scene is perfect and real!!

Silence is the voice we hear,
Peace and serenity is here,
Warmth, Calmness everywhere,
Nature's beauty is so dear.

Feel the freshness in the air,
Blue canopy is so clear and fair!
All day, all night, want to sit and stare,
Nature thy allure is never a glare!!

Palo Alto, California

A Dazzling Day

A Diamond ball spreading daylight?
Looks dazzling and bright!
Glowing silver plate at a height..?
The brilliance is blazing and white!

A crystal ball glistening tight?
Oh! What a magnificent sight!
A golden globe gleaming to entice?
Heaven looks alluring and precise!

Sparkling tapestry spread high?
The glitter is a treat to our eyes!
A radiant lamp illuminating the sky?
End of a perfect day! Without a sigh!

Chennai, India

Marigold

Blooms and shines without a call,
Stands erect, straight and tall!
Brilliant colors make us stall!
Dances and swings like a pretty doll!

Spreads Freshness,and fragrance all around,
Vibrance and exuberance abound,
Nature wears your golden crown!
Your glory is the talk of every town!

Flourish, and adorn a sunny day,
Beaming, cheerfully as you sway!
You ring in festivity and joy, our way,
Merrily you shine in gold, like a little Fay!!

Mt. Robson, Jasper

Mt. Robson

Mt Robson you stand tall and high,
Touching the pretty blue sky!!
Clouds kiss you as they fly by,
Gently you bid them goodbye!

Evergreens watch your summer grace,
As you adorn a bonnet with white lace!
You make passerby pause and gaze,
Oh mighty Mountain, you just amaze!

Your summit is a sanctuary of divinity,
Stately you display your sublimity!
Forging tranquility in your vicinity,
Mt. Robson abode of spiritual Trinity!!

Athabasca Glacier, Canadian Rockies

Canadian Rockies

Expansive mountain ranges,
Jagged peaks on its fringes,
Snow-packed tops with white tinges,
Glaciers carved valleys with granges!

Rivers and lakes sparkle by day,
Grizzlies,elks, moose roam the causeway!
Pines, fir and spruce perform their ballet!
Nature's artistry takes our breath away!!

Mt. Robson stands magnificent and tall,
Crystal waters gushes down Shannon fall,
Can hear Gastown steam clock whistle and call,
Wobbly Capilano bridge makes one sprawl!

Flyover Canada lets you zoom through the sky,
Stanley park awes every passerby,
Confluence of the rivers, a delight to one's eye (s)
Natural bridge, an amazing sculpture no one can deny!!

Glass floor of the Athabasca glacier, a stunner!
Spiral railroad on Rockies an acer,
Sapphire waters of the lake Louis a charmer,
Icefield Skywalk is a true thriller!

Gondola ride, to the peak, a trip to paradise!
Sparkling water down the Spahats falls, a surprise!
Golden summit of Sun peak makes one fantasize,
Roaring waters of Bow falls just mesmerize!!

Ocean Cay, Bahamas

Ship's Deck

Daystar of hope and joy is raising,
Glorious, golden horizon arresting,
Fiery clouds sets the sky blazing,
Oh my! My heart goes racing!

Yellow,orange,and gray begin to interplay,
Whistles,beginning of a magical day!
The dazzling effulgence is sure to stay.
Glistening waters, takes our breath away!

Tranquil sea, a mesmerizing calm,
Gentle breeze, damp and warm,
Ship's deck fills as the cruisers swarm,
Set to capture the picturesque charm!

Caribbean Cruise

Diary of a Cruiser

Day one and two in ship from dusk to dawn,
Day three on the shores of San Juan,
Day four on Virgin Islands by morn,

Day five entered Taino Bay as the sun shone
Day six watched seagulls until they were gone...
Day seven at Ocean Cay ate salad and corn!
Day eight back to Miami shore at the crack of dawn!

Glorious MSC Cruise Ship!!

On the Cruise Ship

Stately Ship sails on to the skipper's command...
Cruisers fill the Atrium with goblets in hand,
Listening to mystic music by the ship's band,
The ship looked gussied up and grand!!

Hot, breakfast in the marketplace,
Theater shows set the stage ablaze,
Pools, water sport, were children's craze
Galleries and shops, the ship was a true maze!

Dazzling lights lit up the ship day long,
Cruisers swayed and danced to the artist's song,
Games and shows went beyond the midnight gong,
There was blithe and mirth all long!!

Mantri, Chennai, India

Dawn

Glorious Dawn greets the day,
Copper hue lights up the bay!
Awning the darkness and gray away,
Spectrum of colors begin their play!

Brilliant orange disc hangs sky high,
Gentle ripples on water, a bit shy!
Sensuous scene stops a passerby,
A breadth taking treat for our eye!

Grays of night about to break,
Creator's creations set to awake!
Ambience and aura are just divine!
Pure tranquility, in the artist's design!!

Mangalore, India

Lilly

Daintily you stand bright and straight,
Grace and elegance you exuberate,
A mystical flash you create,
Your beauty has no equate!

Poise and purity you personify,
Spiritual resurrection you signify!
Swamps and Marshlands you glorify,
Still waters of ponds you sanctify!

You take roots in the fetid,
Nurtured and nourished by fen wetted,
Yet you rise above them tall!
Spread your allure and fragrance to all!

San Jose, CA

Spring Time!

Manors,villas carpeted with blooms!
Goodbye Grays , no more glooms!
Golden poppies, yellow buttercups,
Colorful irises,stand tall and up!

Bright blue skies with streaks of gray,
April showers, trees and plants pray.
Refreshing winds gently blow,
Mountain snow is set to melt and flow!

El Quito Park, San Jose, CA

Lonely Seagull!!

Hi Gull, looking for someone dear?
Missing your loved one that's clear,
Walking listlessly by the lushes near,
Your dismal squawk each day I hear.

Dawns bring promises and hope,
Distress at times are difficult to cope,
Life is transient, angst has no scope,
Cheer up little bird, get set to lope!

Seen your flock by the bay and lake,
See your lonesome at daybreak,
Dear bird, flap your wings,soar high,
New beginning awaits in the blue sky!

Aurora Borealis, Alaska

A Cosmic Delight!

Green, magenta, red and blue !
A mesmerizing light show! It is true!
Watched with eyes simply glued,
What a glorious display! sure to rule!!

Show starts as day fades into night,
Glows until dawn! An amazing sight!
Ballad of twirling lights! A magical delight!
Oh my! Magnificence at great height!

Stood in dark wilderness, to watch,
A celestial exhibit of top notch !
Colorful dancers come in batch,
This heavenly show has no match!!!

Bellrock, Sedona

Sedona

Magnificent orange, red and brown,
Ethereal red cliffs surround the town!
Brightly adorned in layered gown,
Cathedral, Bell rocks form a crown!

Miles and miles of carved red wall,
Grandeur makes a passerby stall!
Mystical sculptures, mighty and tall,
Revere the Creator,who made them all!

Red rocks below magical blue skies,
Twisted junipers catch our eyes!
Spiritual energy felt on points high,
Abode of tranquility no one can deny!

Fairbanks, Alaska

Creator's Seal

Morning star is on the ascend,
As Luna begins her descend,
Lighting up universe in all bends,
Nature dazzles, in the hue it sends!

Bright blue carpet begins to unfold,
Frozen land gets painted in gold!
Trees weighed by snow they hold,
Another glorious day has rolled!

Curtains open to a day surreal,
Scene simply tranquil and real,
Magnificent morning starts with a zeal!
All praise to the creator's seal!

Garden Isle!!

Garden Isle!!

Oh you! Gorgeous Garden Isle!
Draped in emerald vales for miles!
Turquoise waters glisten, and smile,
Mountain spires stand tall in style!

Jagged cliffs, cascading waterfalls,
Red, green canyon stuns one and all!
Coconut palms waves an Aloha call,
Stunning sunrise makes one stall!

Vibrant flowers, fine scents we smell,
Nature's beauty is at its swell!
Cosmic dancer, in a shrine he dwells!
Casts his pure magical spells!

An Alpine Experience

Swiss beauty sensuous and serene,
Enchanting in blue, white and green,
Mystical landscape, never has one seen!
It's splendor, just stunning and clean!

Rhine falls roars, can feel the gush,
Kisses of mist,makes one blush.
Grossmunster church stands up tall!
Zurichsee feeds Limmet and all.

Mt.Titlis soars high up into the sky!
Panorama atop enthralls a passerby
Glistening snow lights the mountain ridge!
A floral kaleidoscope fringe Chapel bridge!

Cogwheel train up to Mt.Jungfrau,
Peak walk suspension sways to and fro,
Ice palace embellished with ice sculptures!
Sphinx tower flaunts Aletsch glacier!!

Crystal studded lakes,dazzle and glow!
Rhine, Aare, and Rhone gently flow,
Cow bells chimes as they graze meadow!
Alps mesmerize with a golden halo!